I0482430

Drawing for beginners

7 steps to be a professional artist
Learn how to draw in one day!

By Amy Hughes

Table of contents

Disclaimer

While all attempts have been made to verify the information provided in this book, the author does assume any responsibility for errors, omissions, or contrary interpretations of the subject matter contained within. **The information provided in this book is for educational and entertainment purposes only. The reader is responsible for his or her own actions and the author does not accept any responsibilities for any liabilities or damages, real or perceived, resulting from the use of this information.**

The trademarks that are used are without any consent, and the publication of the trademark is without permission or backing by the trademark owner. All trademarks and brands within this book are for clarifying purposes only and are the owned by the owners themselves, not affiliated with this document.

Introduction

Drawing has never been made easier, on this comprehensive guide, drawing takes a different twist as you get to learn the most commonly used techniques and how simple and fun drawing can be. Who says drawing has to be tough and complex? Packed with photos and short exercises to direct you, this book is definitely what you need, it can never be easier.

Drawing begun before time, way back centuries ago; from the stone-age to the historical epic times, drawing has been in existence and continues to advance and baffle as time goes by, we have seen some paintings such as the Mona Lisa that is almost a mirage of a high quality camera copy, or coded drawings that have been used to unravel some ancient secrets, drawing has been the best form of communication and also was the first. By following the six steps in the book, you will be advancing to a new communication platform.

Did you also know that drawing is beneficial for your health? It has been proved to help in mind relaxation and also awake the nervous system which later leads to a higher and faster rate of quick thinking, by practicing how to draw you feel relieved and calm.

Drawing can be a hobby; it can be something you do for personal development, it is an activity that you can do during your free time, if done well, you might earn a couple of bucks out of it. By practicing drawing you also develop some life skills that can help you out, you can become a painter, a graphic design artist or venture into many promising careers in art.

Did you know that painters are one of the best problem solvers? They have a unique ability to view all situations in different angles that others cannot, they are open minded people who see what others can't see. They make the best out of worse things and situations.

The best thing about drawing is there is no age limit, as long as a person has the ability to move any part of his or her body parts, they can draw! I have seen the handicapped draw with their legs, with their mouth and also the normal use their bodies to draw, art is everywhere.

You also don't need some special equipment to draw, as said earlier it is not complex or hard to do, all it requires is an imagination, there are so many forms of materials you can use for drawing from sand, to charcoal or pens and pencils. There is no limitation.

By engaging in drawing, you engage yourself in creativity and learning, your mind then becomes super active and open to more information, you then grow smart as you will be curious to learn more and do better.

Drawing is the only form of art that uses telepathy, when you draw, you are putting down what's on your mind for another person to view and get what you're thinking about without talking or sign language, for example when you see a nice portrait of a sunny day and children playing on the field, you can tell that the artist was expressing joy without even talking, or if you see A dark portrait of an abandoned house at night, you can tell the artist either had something scaring him or was gloomy.

Drawing doesn't necessarily have to be as its perceived by many people, it's not hard and stressful, by reading this book, you will be amazed at what you have been missing out, enjoy!

First step

Getting Ready

The first step is to know your tools, you have to identify what is needed to kick off your drawing sessions, the right apparatus will provide quality outcome, hence the need to know what you are going to use and how to choose the best, to start making a list of what you need, first consider the following factors, they are the determinants:

Size of the drawing

If you want your drawings to be large then consider purchasing the materials you will use in bulk to avoid running out. Drawing entails a lot of sketching and rubbing, a single pencil or piece of charcoal won't be enough.

Surface of the drawing

The surface is where you draw, it is where you put down your imagination or figure; it should therefore be as much comfortable as possible to suit your needs. Majority of the beginning artists are recommended to use smooth surfaces while the pros prefer some hard surface like canvas.

Some painting material if you wish to make it colourful

 A little colour will brighten your drawing, but it's not a must you use paint or crayons. Most artists only use colouring apparatus either when they need to put some life in their drawings or when they are dissatisfied with the outcome. If you choose to add some colour to your drawings make sure that the colour you choose blends in, for example if you draw a tree, don't paint it red make it natural and green.

Your budget

Your budget is another factor you should consider; different items have different costs, the type of drawing that you wish to make will determine the apparatus to use, the more complex the drawing, the much apparatus you will use making it costly, for beginners, try out something not too complex at first.

After going through this factors, you now know how much to spend and which type of drawing you want to make. However, you will still need a list of what to purchase, the quantity and quality will be based according to the factors above.

Pencils

Pencils are mandatory in drawing, and not just an ordinary pencil but a pencil with graphite which is erasable with any eraser, pencils usually come in sets where they are arranged as to the lightness or the thickness of the graphite inside, thick pencils don't involve a lot of sharpening but are not accurate in marking, thin pencils are accurate but need constant sharpening.

Sketchbooks

The sketchbook is the secret artist's breeding ground, it is a blank paper page with no margins, comes in a variety of colours, it is where the artist spends most of his time perfecting on what he does best i.e., drawing. It is therefore important to choose a sketch book that you will be comfortable with and attracted to, consider it as your backyard, you will spend more time in your backyard if it's beautiful. However, most artists prefer the ones with the large sheets.

Drawing surfaces

The drawing surface is where you transfer your sketches by drawing from your sketch book, it is where you make the final drawing; it is like an answer book in an exam, apart from that, there are some factors you need to consider while choosing the best suited drawing surfaces, these are:

a. **The weight of the paper**. The heavier the page or sheet seems to be, the complex skills it will require from the artist, the weight of the paper is determined by its ream, a light ream can effortlessly be folded while a heavy one is hard to fold, when purchasing a drawing surface choose the light one at first, it requires less skills hence recommended for the beginner.

b. **The texture of the paper**, also known as the tooth of a paper. If the drawing surface has a rough texture then the drawing might carry some broken lines when it's finished, some artists like it that way but a smooth surface will enhance the value of the drawing.

c. **Resistance of the paper,** also referred to as the acid test, it specifies if a paper can last for long without wearing out in terms of colour and fading off, you probably have come across an old book which was unreadable due to fading off or yellowness, and another old book that is clear as yesterday, you will notice that their papers have different withstanding acidity strength hence one fades off quicker than the other.

Erasers

An eraser is a tool you can't afford not to have, it clears all mistakes. Did you know that there are four different kinds of erasers each with a unique way of erasing? Below are the different types of erasers and how they function.

a. **Plastic eraser**

This type of eraser can remove all sorts of marks on a surface but uses a high amount of friction which can cause damage to the sheet or paper.

b. Gum eraser

This eraser can remove just about anything without damaging the drawing surface; its only disadvantage is that it doesn't erase some materials such as graphite.

c. Rubber eraser

This eraser is the most commonly used; it uses friction to clear off.

d. Kneaded eraser

This is the only kind of eraser that doesn't use friction, it is applied to the surface and sticks to it after which when later pulled, clears the whole surface.

Sharpeners

For sharpening the pencils, can be electric or manual. NB. Make sure it sharpens well.

Charcoal

Charcoal is a good alternative where there are no pencils on sight and also where there is a lot of sketching work to be done.

Art material storage

Where you store your drawings is also a matter of concern, papers especially are prone to all sorts of disasters, whether is water splashed on them or seemly dump humidity, anything can alter with your drawing, to safeguard your drawings you can purchase or make a rolling back to keep your drawings, you can also cover them in polythene to keep them far from moist.

After choosing the right apparatus, you are now ready for the next step. The next step is choosing what you want to draw.

2nd step

Choosing an image

Choosing an image to draw is by far the one of the mentally straining aspects that an artist encounters; you as the artist want your drawing to stand out but at the same time don't want to waste your time and resources working on a complex image that will mess up eventually. That is why it is important to take time on choosing the right especially for beginners.

The right image will please you and challenge you to do other more, that's why it's recommended not to choose something that is too simple. If you work only on what doesn't challenge you, you will never develop much further as you will never be motivated, take time in choosing what to draw, some people already have experience while others don't, don't feel ashamed in making your choice, try out what is average for you.

For beginners, it is recommended that you start off with some simple images and simple apparatus, don't trick yourself and head off to drawing copies of the Mona Lisa and so on, I can feel your excitement and hype which is a good thing, but hold your horses, you don't want to end up messing up and wasting your energy. You can start by drawing a vase with flowers or your house, just to start up the rhythm; you can also choose from the following photos, we shall draw them step by step till your drawing looks just as they appear.

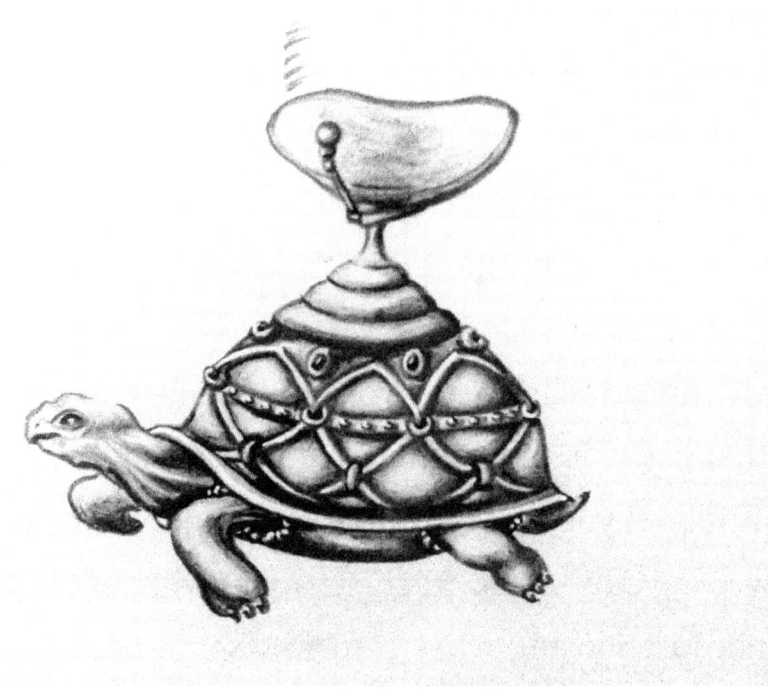

This photo of a tortoise with a satellite dish is not as hard as it looks like; you will be amazed at how simple it is to draw, there are also some more you can choose from below, keep in mind that nothing is impossible in the artists eye, you have to believe in yourself and push your mind to pursue.

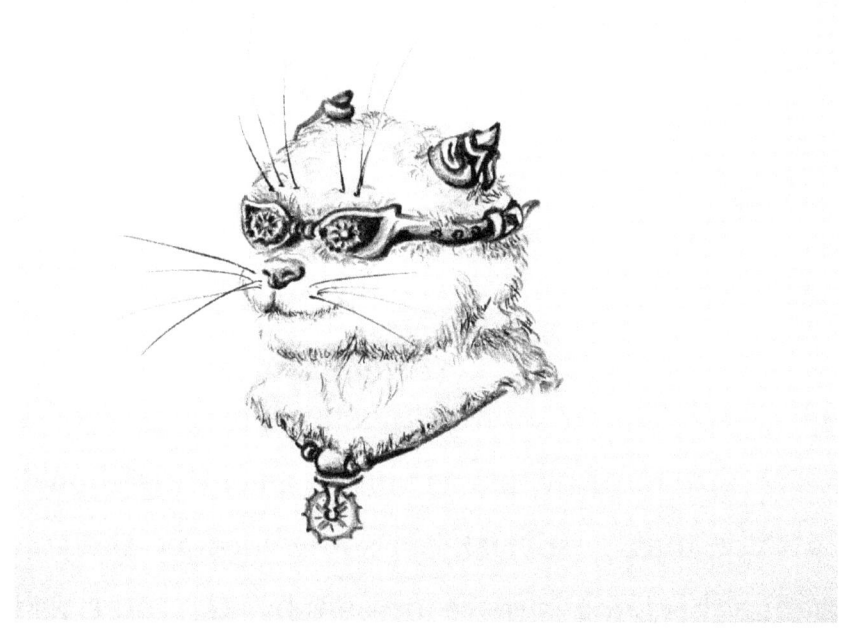

You can also choose this one, it simpler than you think and will not consume much time, plus doesn't have a lot of sketching.

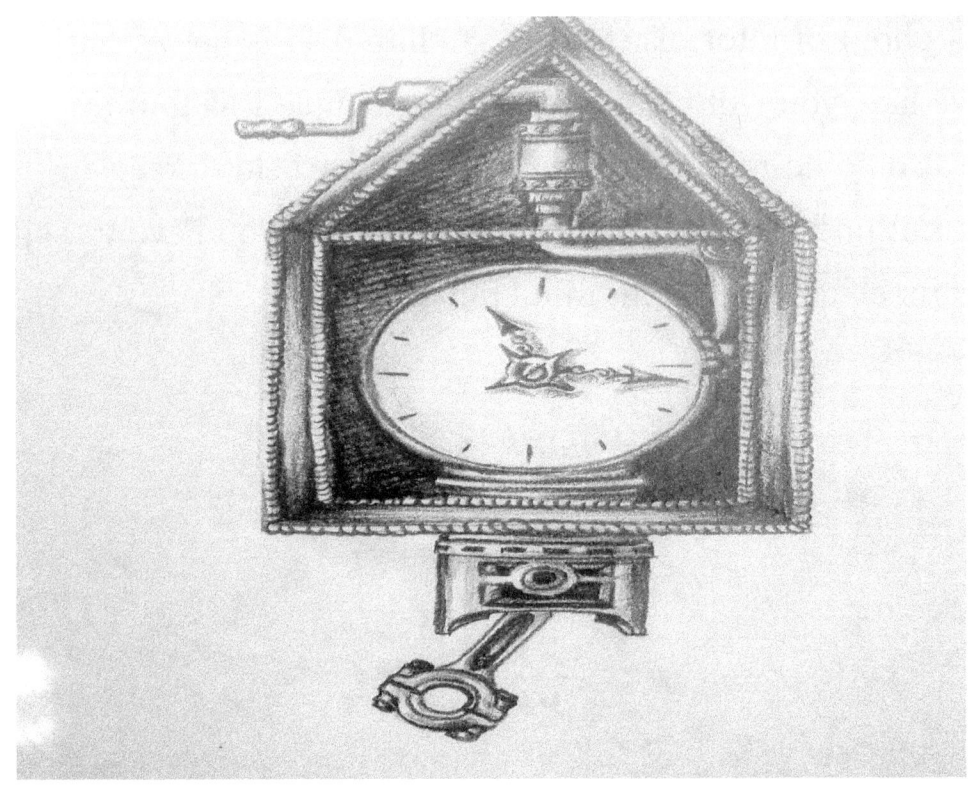

The clock photo is one of the most popular images that the beginners choose to draw, it's as simple as cutting though a cake but can also be tough especially in some corners, the good thing about reading this book is there are step by step tutorials to teach you.

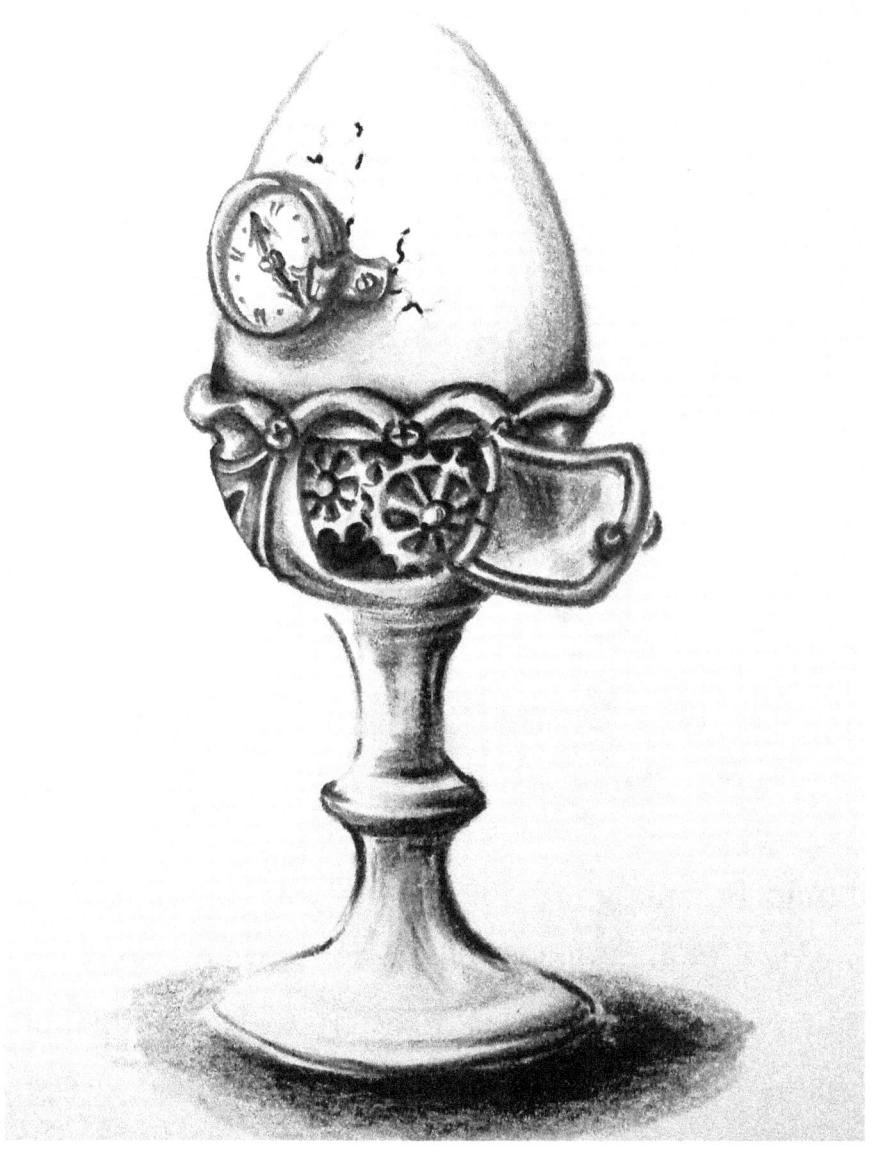

The egg with a watch on a vase was actually drawn live in a classroom, the artists claimed that by organizing and planning which parts to draw first, they found it amazingly simple than imagined, it can be the hardest image to sketch and draw especially the corners and sketching but when you plan how to draw it, it will be a success.

Here is another one you can try out:

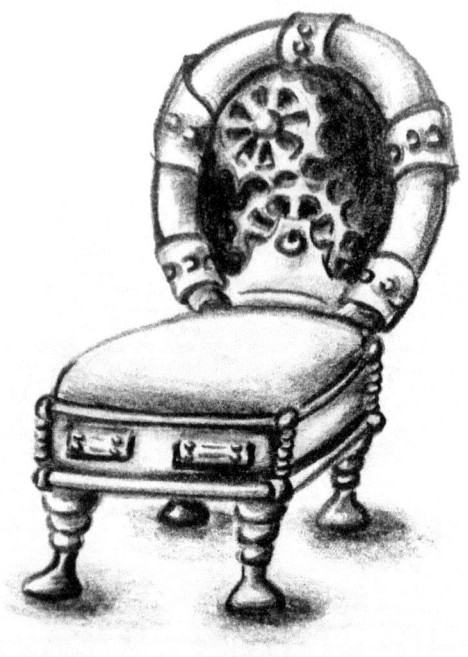

That should be enough challenge for you to think of, you also have the freedom to look for your own figure or landscape, don't limit your potential. As you can see from the photos above, the artist has used either charcoal or thick pencil, the drawings are basic and not as tough as they look, over the next steps you will learn from step one, how the artist drew these images.

3rd Step

The Outline

You now have your drawing set comprising of the apparatus mentioned in the earlier chapter. You also have figured out what to draw and why it is a good start for you, now we move to the practical.

Don't forget:

Drawing involves having some know-how on the different kinds of pencil and charcoal techniques, without having any knowledge on these techniques; you are bound to waste time and resources. Consider yourself as an aeroplane engineer; you can't fix a plane if you don't know how it works. It is therefore very important to be keen as we go step by step to making the final drawing. The techniques are of great value because they help in making the work easier plus enable you to identify which technique is appropriate for your drawing or a certain part of the drawing so as to make it more attractive.

Have your pencils sorted out first of all, if possible make sure that the pencils you have are from one company and are in variety with different grades, after getting your pencils together, take out your mini sketchbook and flip the first page, note a sketchbook should be in minimal size so that it can easily fit in your pocket or bag in this matter.

The main purpose of a sketchbook is to practice drawing, remember that drawing is an art and all sorts of art require lots of practice, a mini sketch book will help out in all areas, you can draw from anywhere, the cafeteria or the bus or at the field, instead of carrying your drawing surface which can be tiresome or uncomfortable.

The first technique involved is the outline

The outline is basically the outer garment of the drawing; it is the coat of the drawing as most artists refer, the outline is the shape of your drawing and should always be the first thing you draw, the outline will help you in assessing the space you need and curving the tight angles before actually drawing, to do this you will need a light grade pencil and a heavy grade pencil, take a look below at the examples:

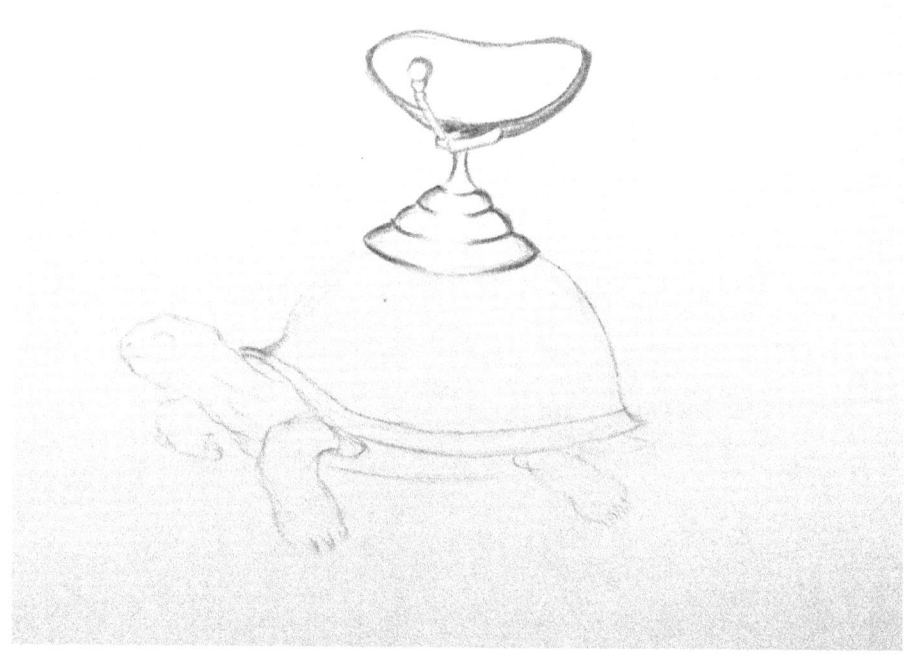

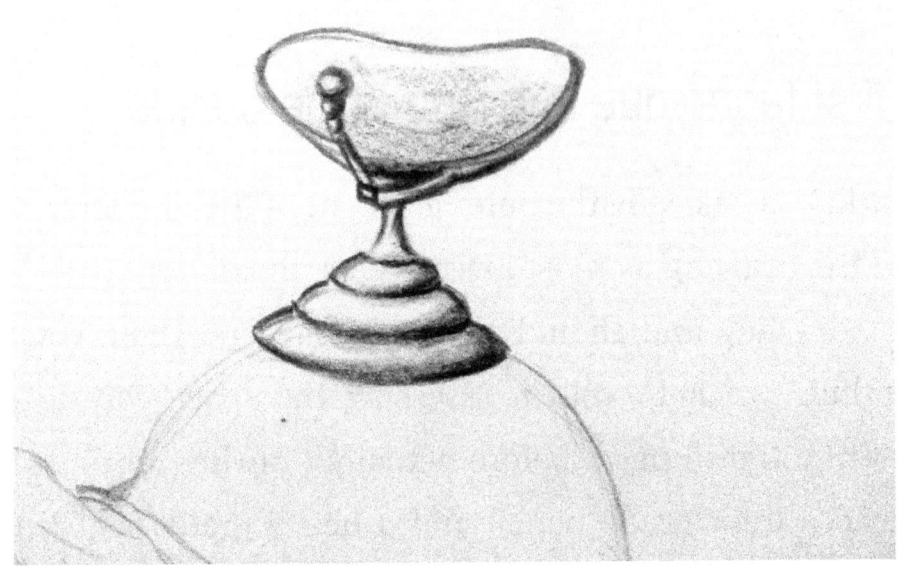

The photos above are the outlines for the tortoise with a satellite, look closely and study them, here are other examples.

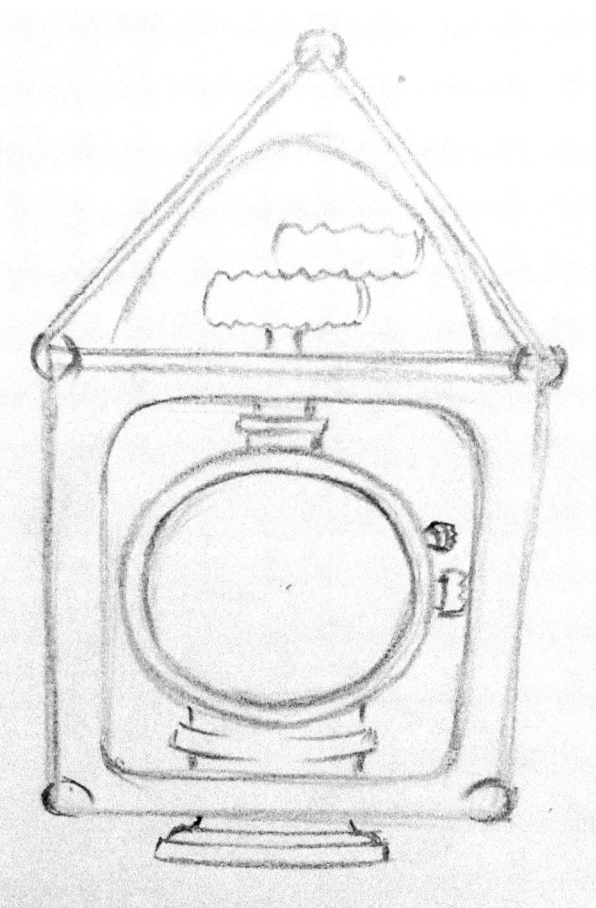

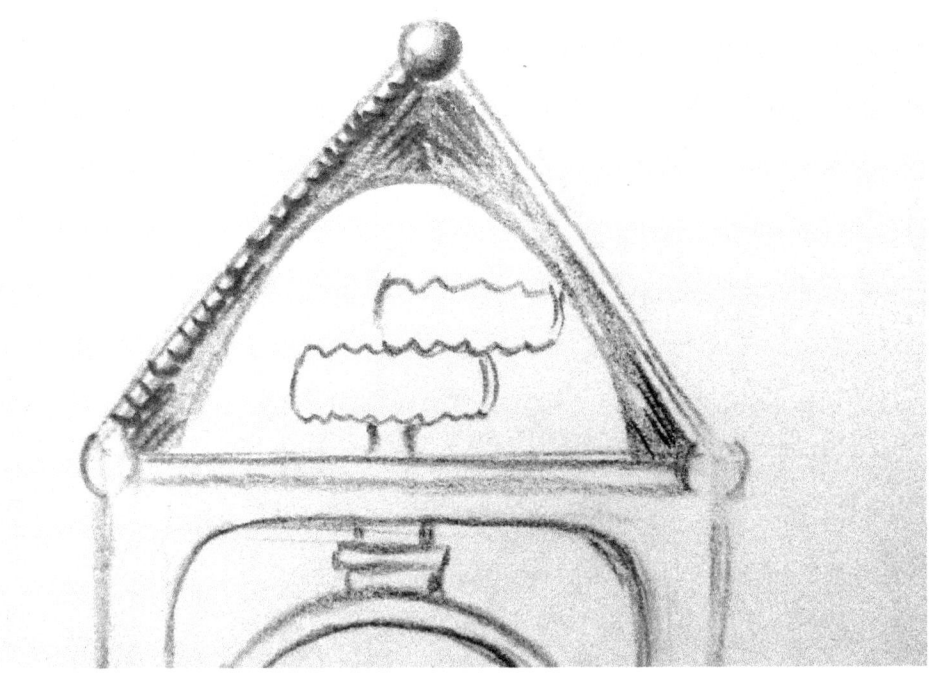

If you flip back to the second chapter, you will notice that the images seem to be more complex and skilfully drawn but the diagrams included above and below seem easy when only the outline is done. This is because the outline is more of the skeleton, it lacks only twenty per cent of the drawing, check the other images below and come up with your observations.

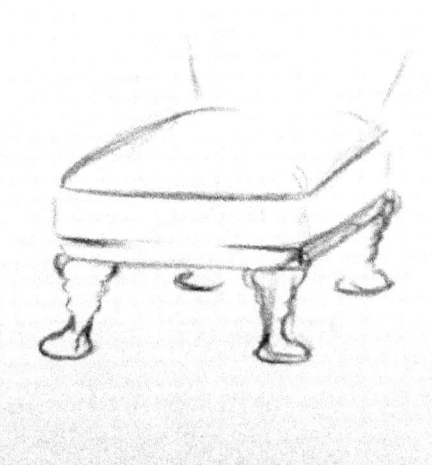

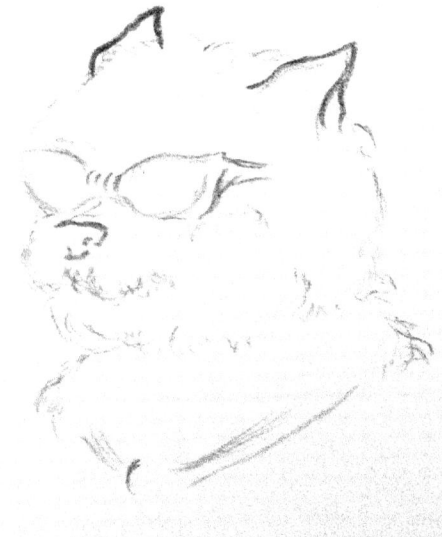

When making your observations, you will notice that the outlines are thin and not continuous; you also notice that the pencil or piece of charcoal that was used to draw was light and sharp. Try this out, using two grades of pencils, that is the thin one and the thick one; sharpen each of this pencils then scribble on a page with less force, you will notice that the thick pencil scribbles thin lines while the thin one scribbles heavily taken into consideration that you used the two with the same amount of pressure.

Instructions on drawing the outline

1. First of all, sit strategically where you have a clear view of the image your drawing. This will help in relaxing and also avoiding the straining that will lead to quick fatigue.

2. Sharpen your pencils

3. Have your sketchbook ready, you can use your lap as the surface if you are not near any support. Having a surface is ideal since you won't keep changing to a position that will fit right in search of comfort.

4. After following the above instructions, take your light pencil and then draw the outline in faint lines. Faint lines will help you in curving the corners and also will be easy to erase where mistakes are made. As you can see from examples of the drawings above, you will notice that there are light lines under the thick lines, this light lines guide the thick lines in creating a more firm outline. The light lines also make the drawing come alive i.e., the drawing becomes natural. You can use these faint lines to your

advantage especially when drawing people or animals, the detectives and other intelligent units use this method to their advantage.

5. After making the light lines, join them together using the thick pencil to form a visible and thicker outline, use much pressure when doing this but don't go overboard and damage your sketchbook with tears or holes.

Other precautions you should know about

a. Always wash your hand before drawing. This is to avoid stains and untidiness, some stains such as oil can ruin your drawing and sketchbook. Dirt will make your work loose quality and value.

b. Avoid getting creases on your drawing board, creases will show up when the drawing sheet is folded in another way than rolling. Creases can tear your drawing sheet or make it bumpy which then will damage the quality of the drawing sheet.

c. Don't lean on the drawing surface, might as well spoil your hard work, be careful when drawing, and your work will amaze you.

d. Don't draw hurriedly as your outline will be haphazardly done. A disfigured outline will be un-satisfactory; it will mislead the whole drawing concept then lead to repeating the whole job again. Take time especially if you are a beginner; have in mind that great drawings took weeks, months and even years.

e. Keep in mind that the outline is the skeleton of the whole drawing, therefore concentrate as much as possible on drawing it well, be specific about the length and height of the drawing you want to draw then draw the outline, if the outline is straight, you can use a ruler to draw.

After realigning the faint lines into thick lines your drawing should now look like these photos:

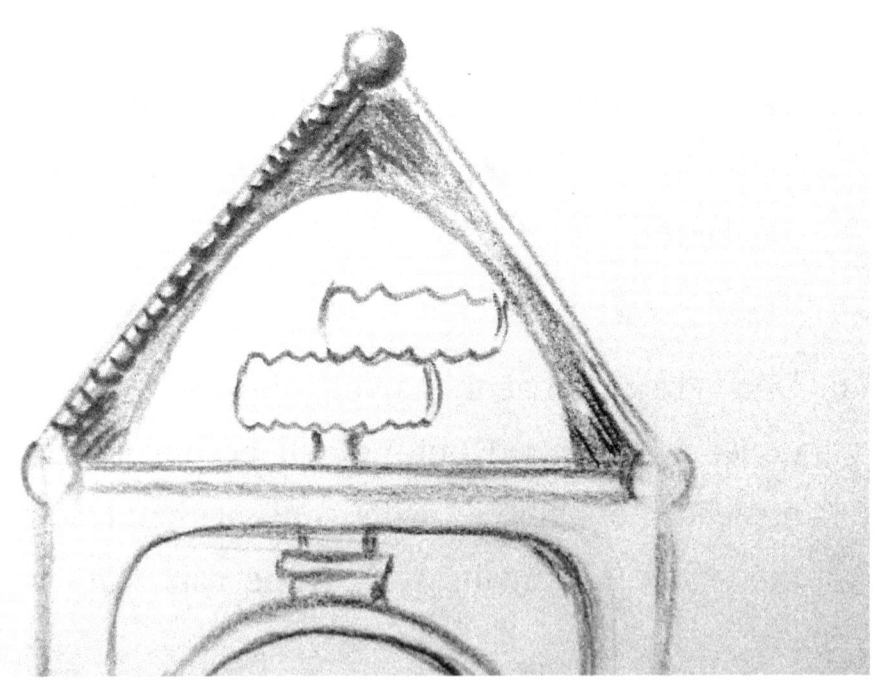

Notice how the lines seem to be thicker than the first photo; this is the effect of the thick outlining with the thick pencil. Check out this other ones.

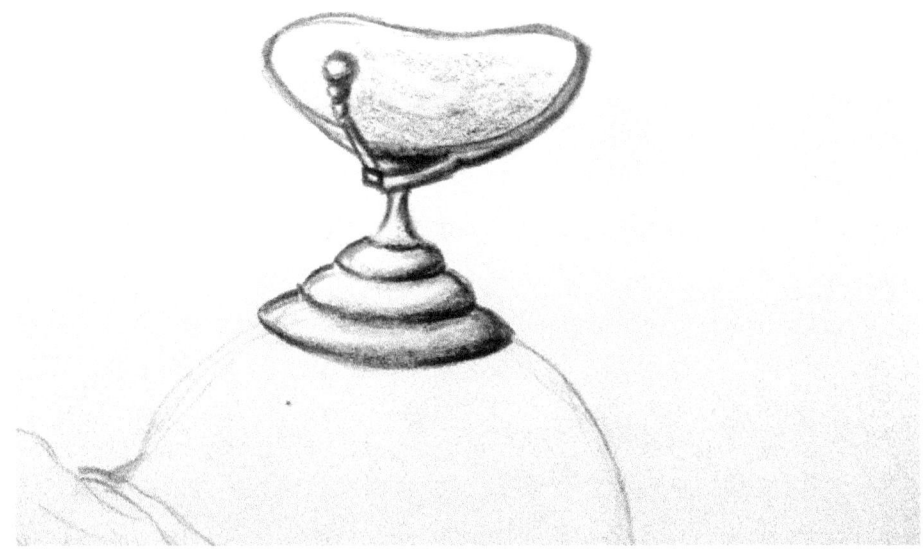

Notice the thick lining over the faint lines? That is the true original outline of the image. It covers the faint lines; remember that the faint lines were only meant to direct the thick lines. Check this out:

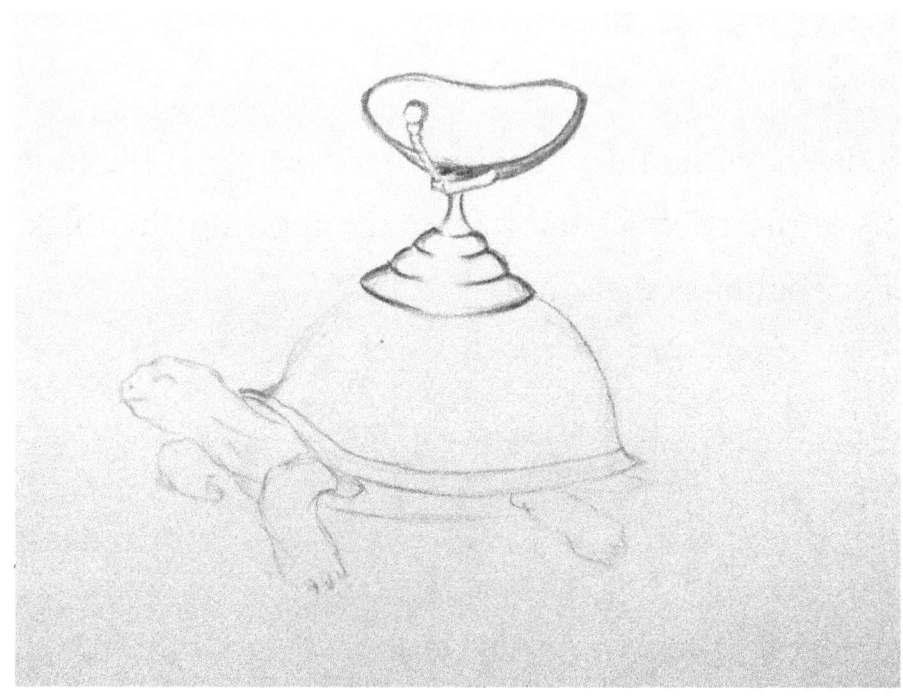

The faint marks are no longer visible; the outline is clear and straight.

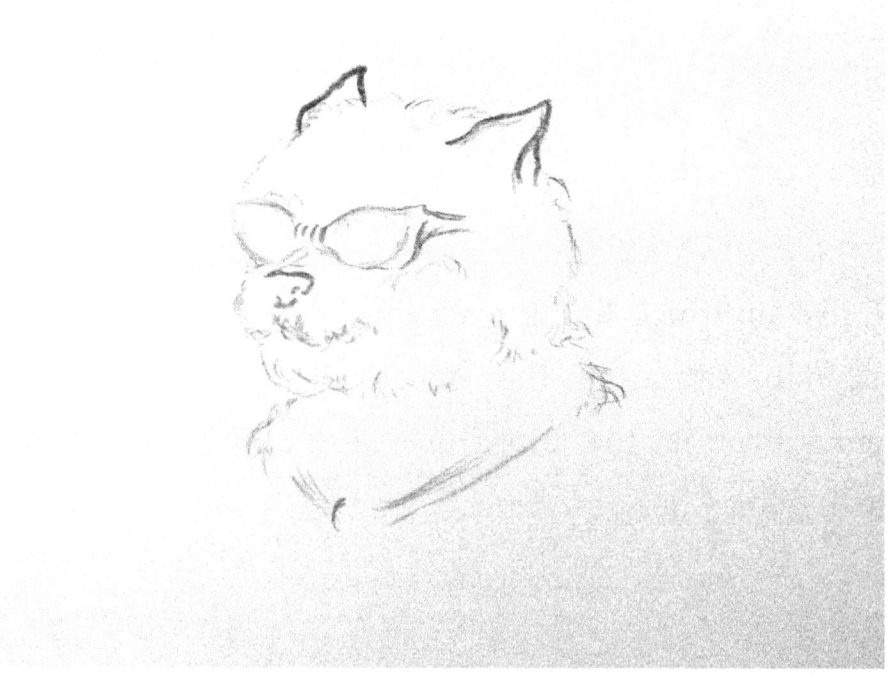

The outline should always be the first thing to draw; it's considered as the foundation of drawing, just like a house with no strong foundation is bound to collapse, the same applies to drawing, whether it's a structure or building, it would collapse without getting finished. Practice drawing outlines on many things and you will soon be a master of it.

Short exercise

Get an item that you can easily draw, maybe a fruit or a jug or something, you might even want to try out a photo on a magazine, draw what you picked up using the outline-first style and see how you do it, get some feedback from friends of your drawing. Try other more images and check the difference, you should have now mastered how the concept is done.

4th step

Hatching and all its different forms

Hatching is how you sketch lines in the same order following the same direction as the image, it is commonly done when drawing the outline with the main intention of making the drawing seem more real and natural. Hatching will add value and glamour to your drawings, picture this, some two young boys are playing with a ball. One of the boys accidentally kicks it with much force till it flies high heading for a nearby window, the boys stand surprised holding their breath as they know they will be in trouble or will have their ball taken away from them. Now there are three things in this scenario that you might want to add to your drawing to make it seem even more real and tell the moment like it happened.

One is there is surprise; you can draw one of the boys looking up as the ball flies in mid-air while the other stares at the ground in disbelief.

Two there is worry, the boys are worried of the outcome; therefore the drawing must express worry and anxiety.

Three; the drawing must have some symbolised movement, it can't just be a still photo, the boys were in the moment of playing and a still drawing can't prove this.

The best thing to do in such a scenario would be to draw the photo by hatching; here are some facts about hatching.

Facts about Hatching

1. **Hatching will make your drawing impressive and attractive**

Hatching is the drawing of lines close together in one direction to form a shape, take for example the old white and black comics of the newspaper; they seem impressive and attractive and even speak by themselves with no need of words.

2. **Hatching brings out the realness and natural essence of a photo**

If you want to draw a bouncing ball, you can't draw its outline straight, it will lack the motion part of it, try hatching its outline and you will be surprised, hatching makes the drawing come alive, as I usually phrase it, " it's like drawing in motion."

3. **Hatching saves time, energy and resources in shading**

Hatching involves drawing lines together, crossed lines together and other ways, while shading involves continuous scribbling till there is no line visible, it's more of covering or painting, shading takes consumes a lot of time while hatching is just marking with lines hence no time loss, it also doesn't require a lot of resources like shading.

4. By hatching, you save yourself from constant erasing and rubbing

Hatching is just the art of drawing lines in different ways, by using this different ways; you get an advantage of hiding over your errors, the drawing of lines close together will cover up that sharp corner you made or that over scribbling you did.

5. Hatching reveals the motion in the photo

Whether it's in comic books, cartoons, long portraits or signs, you will notice that there is much use of hatching where movement is involved, hatching breaks the staunch corners, stability and one way curves of an image, if you look at a drawing made by hatching and another straight, you will notice that one is still while the other isn't.

Different Forms of Hatching

1. Side by side hatching.

Also referred to as parallel hatching, involves drawing lines alongside each other in parallel form that they end up looking like many elevens, side by side hatching is always used where a shadow or a bit of darkness is needed to improve the value and essence of the drawing. Where a bit of darkness or shade is needed, the lines are not drawn close together, where a dark shade is needed, the lines are drawn close together.

2. Contour Hatching

Contour hatching is how lines are drawn side by side and over or underneath each other according to the image's shape or better yet it contours, a contour is simply the landscape shape. Contour hatching is similar to side by side hatching but only differs with drawing lines as according, to the shape of the image.

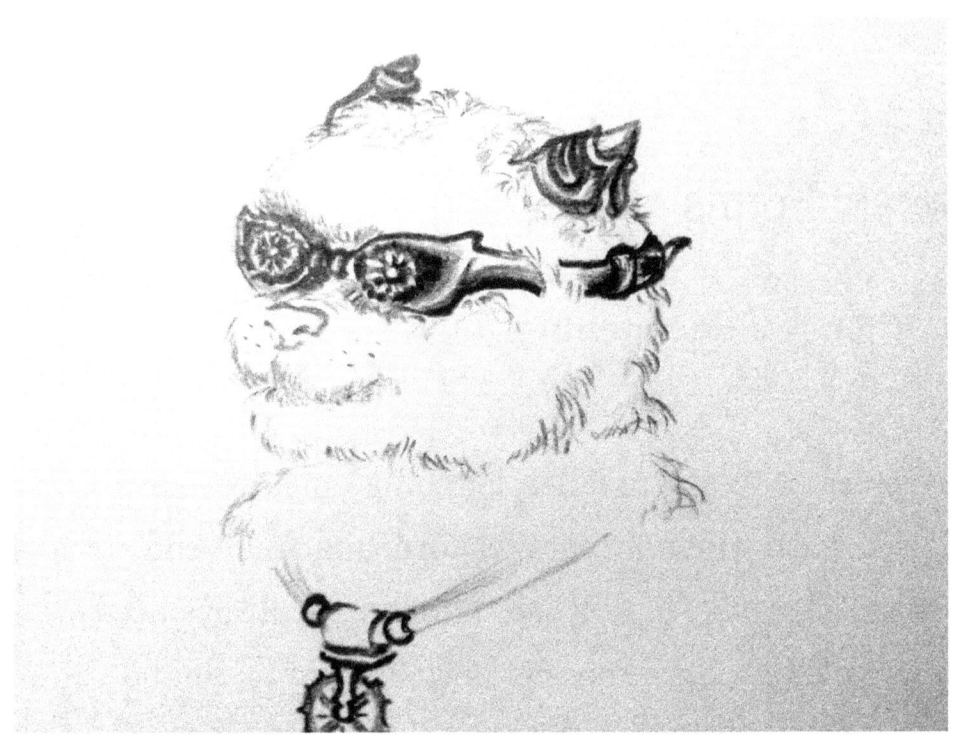

This photo depicts an example of contour hatching technique; the technique has been used to bring out the fur around the cats spectacles.

3. Cross hatching technique

Cross hatching is the simplest technique and also the most common among artists, it involves first of all making either the side by side hatches or the contours hatches diagonally then crossing them with similar lines from the opposite direction making small diagonals, the technique is used to express the opacity of an image or rather enhance some shade but not scribbling, the more you as the artist makes this cross hatches, the darker it becomes. Have a look at his photo below:

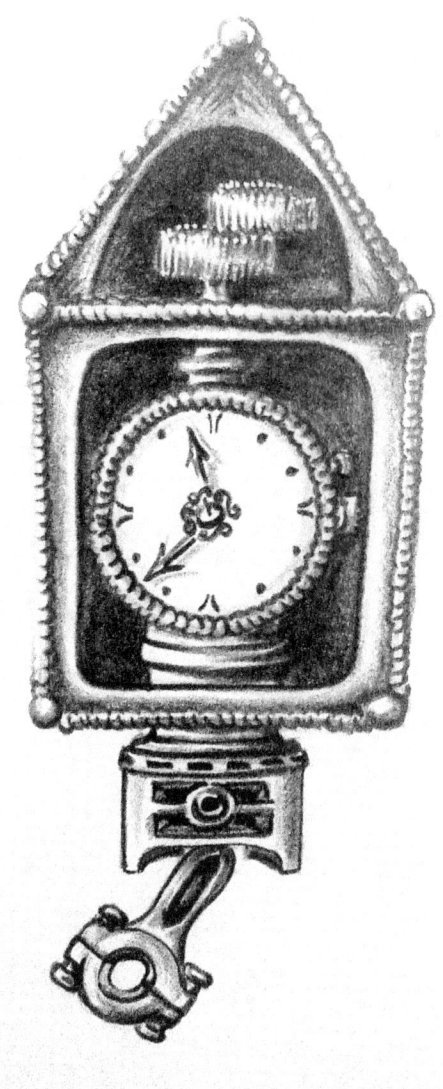

between the circular clock and the house shape, a lot of cross hatching has been done, it has been done with a heavier pencil of a higher grade hence the immense shade.

4. Fine cross hatching

The technique resembles the cross hatching technique except for the fact that in this technique, a variety of different pencils are used. There are faint marks on some portions and also some thick portions on different areas, the main reason for using this technique would be if the artist wants to add value to his drawings by creating an effect of a three dimension image.

5. Mosaic hatching

Also known as the basket or woven hatching technique, is formed by hatching a group of lines crossing against each other diagonally to form a tire like shape, the technique is complex to most as it requires great skill, when drawn it brings out the roughness in a drawing and also meant to bring out the art part of it as well.

Remember the much practice you do, the more your skills develop and the easier and quicker it will be to draw.

Short exercise

Draw your hand on your drawing surface then use the different styles you just read about hatching, this should help you acquire more understanding of the difference between the different forms, remember that drawing entails doing more practical than only reading.

5th step

Circling drawing techniques

The style that you choose will play a role in the quality of your drawing, a blend and touch of well mixed styles will bring out a masterpiece, over the previous chapters, you have learnt about the outline, hatching and different apparatus for the right position, now it's time to learn about the common way of shading and drawing inside the outline.

Drawing inside the outline is less vulnerable to destruction than the outline. I t can also be fun if you make it; here you get the chance to add any effect without ruining the quality of the photo as compared to the outline. Drawing the inside will bring out the emotion and caption of the photo, it will fill the other half of the image.

Basically drawing inside will involve, shading, encircling and a bit of hatching to either bring out the three dimension structure or show where the light is coming from, for example if you draw a hand you will hatch on the palms and fingers just to create that effect that the sun is shining from the opposite palm.

Circling involves shading an image partially and uniformly while the hatching technique involves shading uniformly into small diamonds, unlike hatching which bring out a texture, dimension and feeling about the drawing, the circling technique brings out the natural part of the drawing, for example if you draw a tree, circling will be the best option rather than shading or hatching that will make its glamour vanish. Here are some facts about circling:

1. Brings out the natural essence

The natural essence of the image is the ability of the image to depict nature and also convince the viewer; for example a drawing of a tree bended to one side because of being blown by a strong wind. If you shade the tree with a fixed colour or hatch it, it will portray a different meaning than intended but if you draw by encircling, the viewer is able to get the original meaning by just looking.

2. Time and resource saving

Circling needs no special skills or abilities; you just take your pencil and start drawing, it takes less time since you skip the outline part of the image and also don't have to uniformly shade or scribble plus its much faster and less tiresome.

3. Can substitute hatching in some areas

Especially where pitch darkness is required, Circling will scribble till its dark, also circling can be deployed where the drawing is too big and will consume match time in hatching or drawing outlining, most artists prefer to it than hatching because of this reason, you can also bend a pencil or piece of charcoal to grasp a larger surface area. Have a look at this photo:

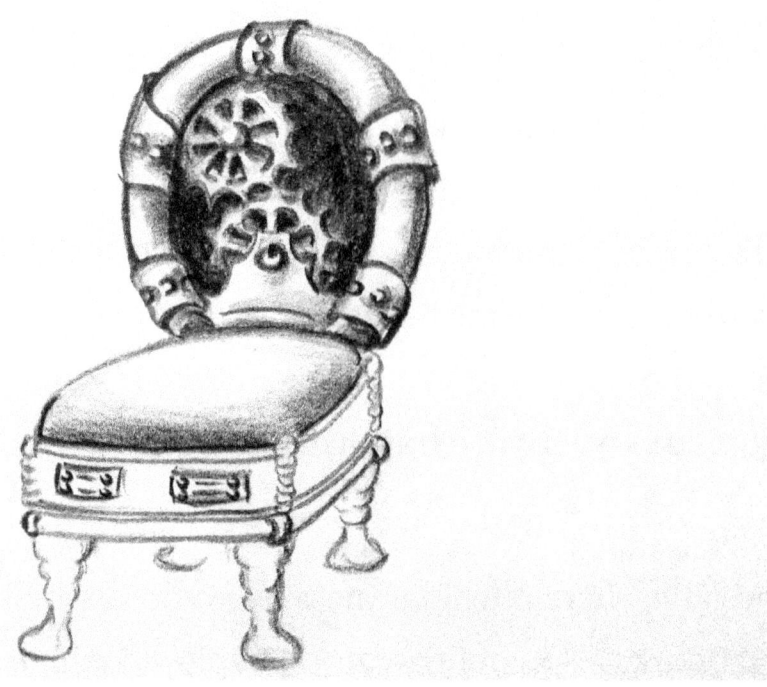

Look closely and observe how the gears and the chair frames are shaded, the artist has used the circling technique here with two different pencils of different grades, the thick one and the thin one, the circling has been done to naturalize the photo.

Short exercise

Get a flower garden photo or go to a nearby flower garden and test what you just read about the circling technique, by now you should be able to draw a bush by simply encircling.

6th step

Shading

After learning about the different styles that incorporate to make a fine drawing, you are almost set to show off your finished project, the final step is shading, now try to imagine how a drawing would be if it wasn't shaded, the diagrams below represent the difference between shaded and un-shaded drawings:

Not shaded:

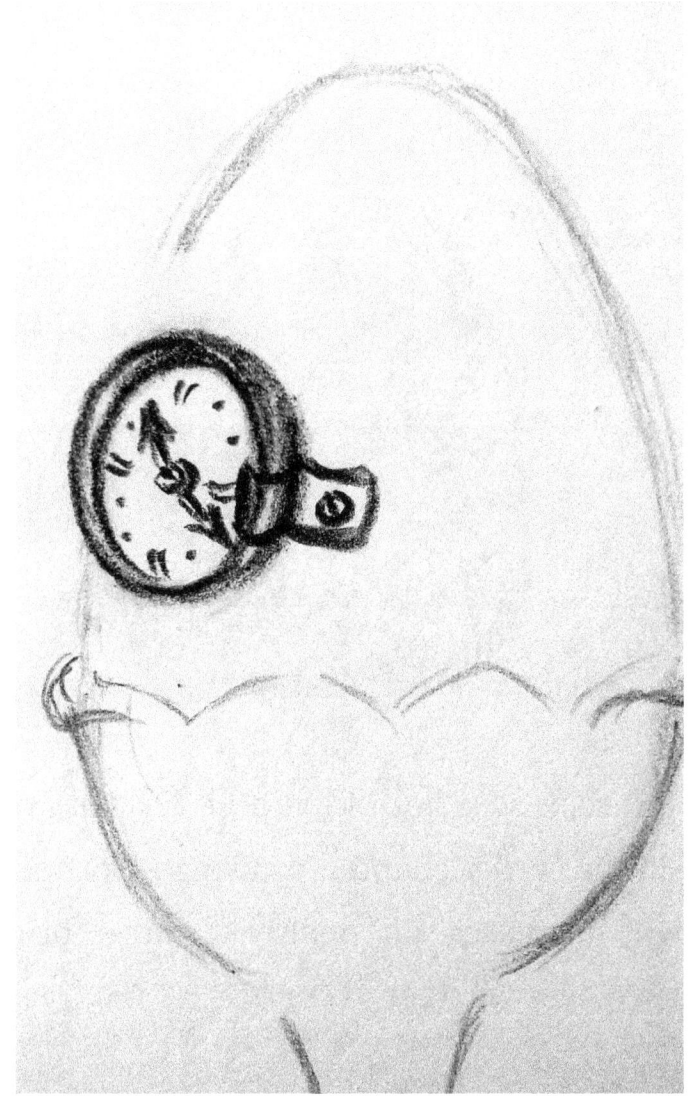

Shaded:

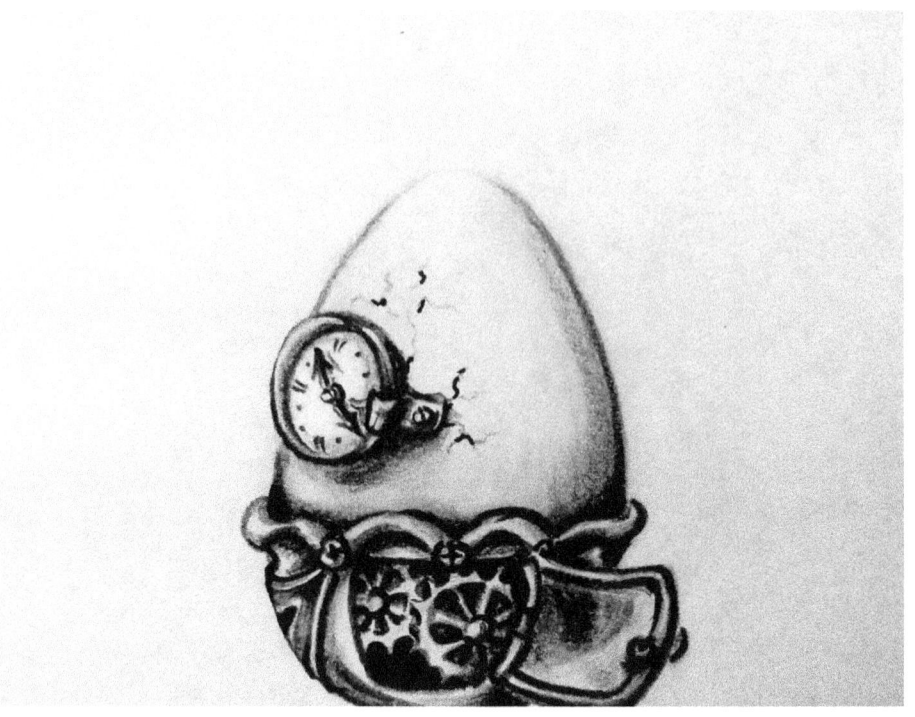

Shading should represent both light and darkness on an image, as described in the earlier chapter, drawing a portrait that has its source of light increases its quality. It also brings out the dimension aspect of it whether 3D or 2D.

There are two forms of shading involved in drawing

1. **Smooth or easy shading**

Smooth shading involves taking your hard pencil and drawing light lines in a zigzag manner close together, the artist uses this style in drawings that don't require much darkness or dim for example a reflection of the sun on the sea. When using this technique use a faint pencil that is not to sharp, also don't put much tension between your thumbs; ease your fingers while holding the pencil to avoid any hard sketching. Check the diagram below:

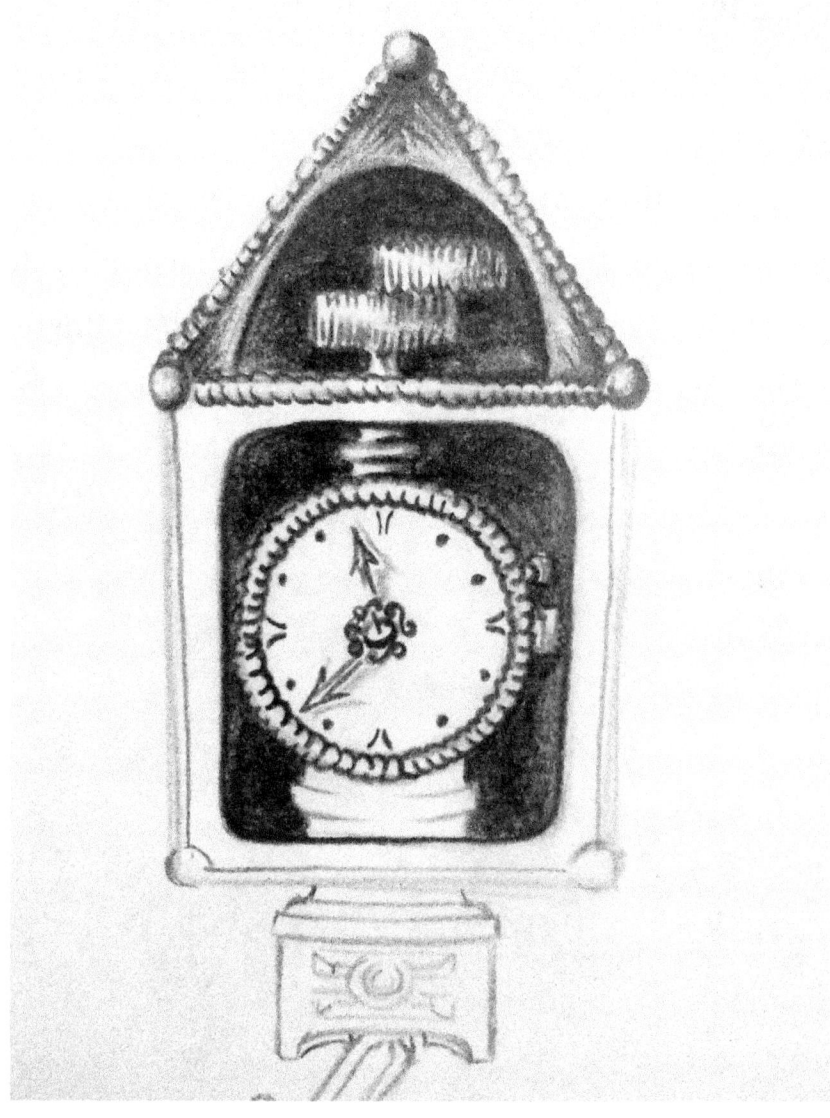

You will notice that the left part of the photo is lighter than the right, the left side has been smoothly shaded.

2. Hard or rough Shading

Hard or master shading is adopted where the drawing needs a lump sum of darkness, for example if the artist is drawing a dark forest or anything that is pitching black. Rough shading is also used to describe the tough structure and texture of the drawing. When using this technique, choose a high grade pencil that will bring out the darkness, hold your pencil in such a way that it won't slide of and spoil the alignment, a bad alignment will look like a big mistake that you don't want. Here is an example of a well hard shaded drawing:

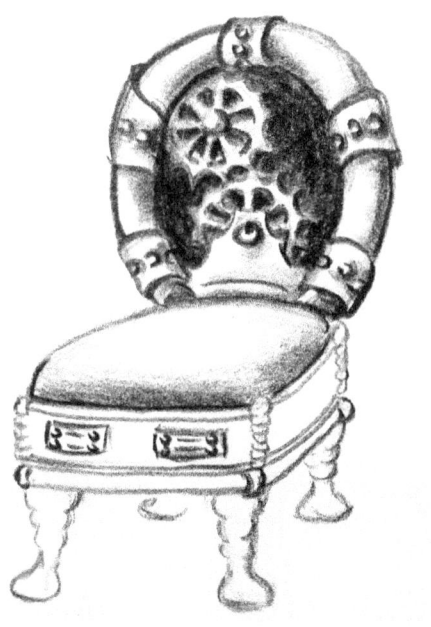

You will notice that the edges are shaded thickly, this is because thick represents the tension that is there.

To build up a shadow whether a light one or a pitch dark one, scribble from the opposite direction on top of your first shadow till it's completely covered.

Short exercise

Place an apple on the table then place a torch at a 30degree angle above it, switch on the torch that it may reflect the apple's shadow to the table, now try drawing it in this position. After that move the torch closer to the apple at the same degree and draw it. You should have to drawings of two different shadows

Practice makes perfect, the more you practice this techniques the more your drawings become more unique and valuable, remember to take time in drawing, don't be hasty, you will be surprised that some of the best drawings took years and years to finish

7th step

Practice images

You are now ready to venture off as a new artist; the world is waiting to see you make your mark, remember that drawing can take to places you only dreamt off, you will reach those from far away and speaking in different languages that you can't understand, you will be an inspiration to many. Practice the images below and also get more complex with time, drawing is fun!

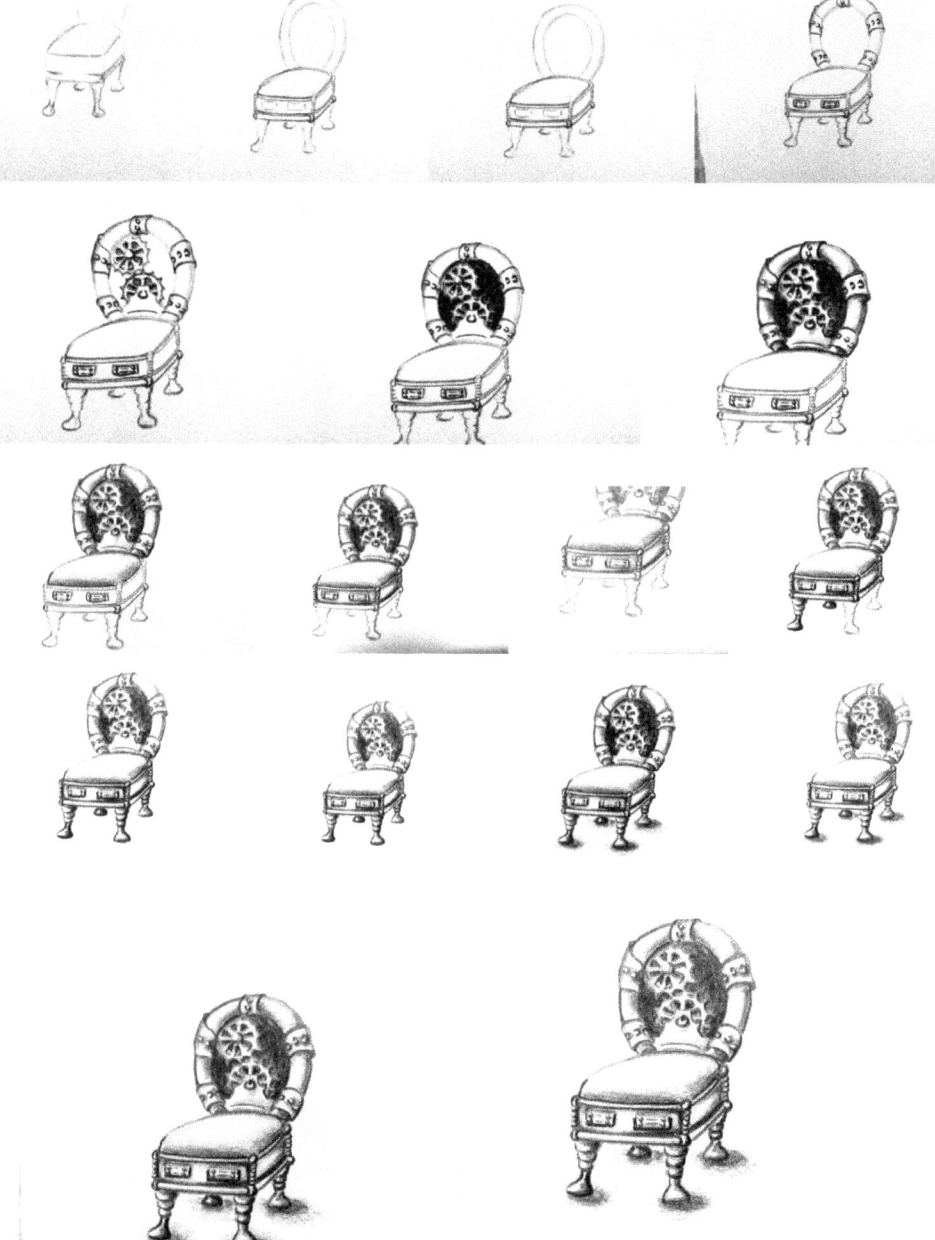

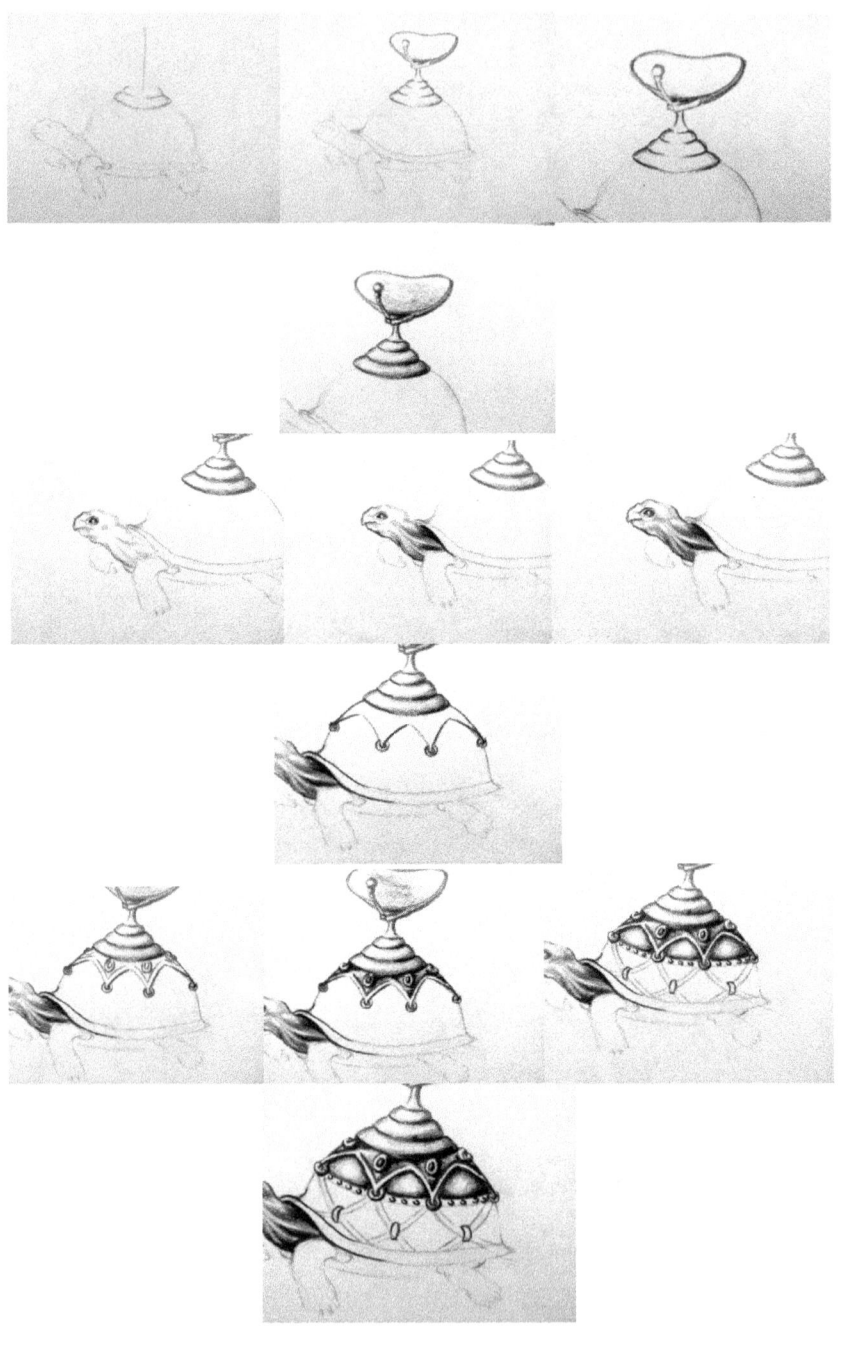

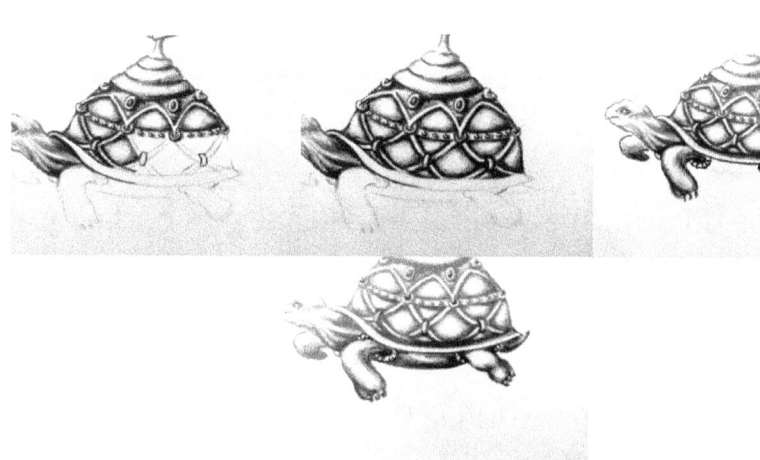

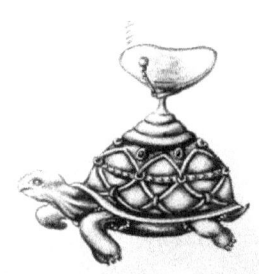

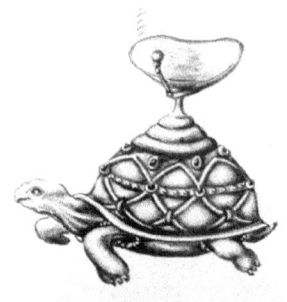

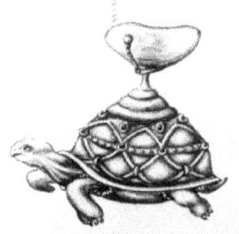

Conclusion

Thank-you for buying this book, I hope that you had as much fun reading as I did writing. After going through the entire book, there is no doubt that you are now fully skilled as an artist to begin your drawing expeditions, the skills and examples in this book will empower you and guide you to the most complex of portraits you wish to draw, you will also discover a new and intriguing colourful world you have never experienced and also sharpen your way of thinking and positivity.

Drawing has been there since existence of time, it was there even before language, the early people used to communicate by drawing on the walls or on the ground; it was then practised by the historical age in the epic times as a decoration to either the king's palace or any royal home. Drawing has since been under continuous development as technology has been enhanced, it has played a major role in the development of the world to where it is today thus being ranked the same as history.

By learning to draw, you are acquiring a new way of expressing yourself and communicating your message, apart from that, if your drawings turn out to be impressive, you might earn a quick buck out of it, as one of the most promising careers at this age, you are bound to achieve more than getting your message through.

Drawing is also a form of anger and stress cure, when you draw, you are venting out your rage or 'heavy-burdens' on concentration. You are then able to concentrate on what really matters most and get some relaxation time.

Over the years drawing has progressively dominated technology, it has now become easier to draw than ever before; we have tablets and phones that support drawing as compared to the past. We have the convenience of the entire universe at our fingertips; we can share our work to the world with just one tap. However, as much as we enjoy these amenities, there is also the negative part of it, drawings are sensitive and a single drawing could be interpreted more than a thousand times differently from how you planned.

I hope to see your drawings on the media soon, be sure of it, the book has been thoroughly researched and well organized to make it as simple as it can ever be to learn how to draw, the styles and plots mentioned have been used by the best artists in the world, they have been adopted to make some of the best drawings there are out there. Be sure to check out my other books as they will also be of great significance to you.

www.ingramcontent.com/pod-product-compliance
Lightning Source LLC
Chambersburg PA
CBHW080539190526
45169CB00007B/2557